Deborah Lee Rose

Ocean Babies

illustrations by
Hiroe Nakata

NATIONAL GEOGRAPHIC

WASHINGTON, D.C.

Big as a bus,

and smaller than seeds,

billions of babies are born to the ocean.

One by one,

and in huge bunches,

they wriggle and spurt from their
mother's body—

or their father's!

Some are born live, like you were.

Even more hatch from eggs.

Ocean babies can look
exactly like their parents,

or completely different.

As soon as they're born,
some already know how to swim.

Others need to learn.

Alone or together,

ocean babies travel far to find food...

or wait for food to find them.

Some change homes
like you change clothes.

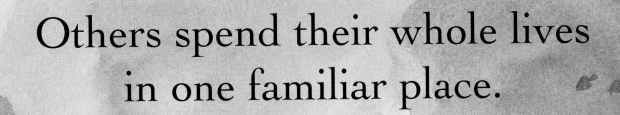

Others spend their whole lives
in one familiar place.

No matter where they live,

what color, shape, or size,

one day ocean babies grow up,
just like you will.

Then, big as a bus,
and smaller than seeds,

billions of *new* babies
are born to the ocean —

and life begins again.

Big as a bus,
Blue whale calves are the ocean's biggest babies. At birth, they're already 20 feet long and weigh 6,000 pounds. A baby blue stays with its mother for two years, living at first on her thick milk. With few blue whales spread across the world, this great species is in danger of disappearing.

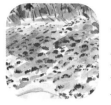

and in huge bunches,
Masses of baby red crabs start life in the sea, then emerge from the water onto Australia's Christmas Island. They burrow for years in the floor of the island's rain forest. When they're finally big enough, the red crabs migrate back to the beach, where females shed their eggs into the ocean.

and smaller than seeds, billions of babies are born to the ocean.
One night each year, soon after a full moon, coral reefs send clouds of eggs and sperm swirling into the warm ocean. These join and grow into new coral polyps, the tiny animals whose hard, outside skeletons create all kinds of coral and coral reefs.

they wriggle and spurt from their mother's body—
Dolphin babies are born underwater, head first or tail first. Since all mammals, including dolphins, need air, dolphin mothers quickly nudge their newborns to the ocean surface for their first breath. After that, a baby and mother swim very close to each other, so the baby is carried along in its mother's watery trail, or "slip stream."

One by one,
Marine mammals like seals, whales, dolphins, walruses, and otters usually have one baby at a time. Harp seal pups born on the Arctic ice stay warm under thick, snowy white fur. Within a few weeks of their birth, they no longer drink their mother's milk but learn to dive for their food in the icy water.

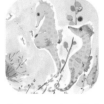

or their father's!
Baby sea horses pop from their father's pouch, where their mother first laid them as eggs. The only fish that swim "standing up," sea horses can hide themselves the way chameleons do, by changing color to blend in with their habitat.

Bat rays are born rolled up like soft tacos and gradually spread out their wing-shaped fins to glide through the water. During birth, the baby's poisonous stinger stays rubbery so it can't harm the mother. After a few days, the stinger becomes hard and deadly.

Even more hatch from eggs.

To lay their pearl pink eggs, sockeye salmon swim thousands of miles from the ocean to the freshwater streams, rivers, and lakes where they were born. Here, baby salmon "fry" spend the first part of their lives in safety. Then they head out for a life at sea until they're ready to spawn their own young.

Ocean babies can look exactly like their parents,

Orca calves are miniatures of their elders—fierce hunters who attack their prey in the waves and even up on the beach. Yet young killer whales face their own dangers and can get stranded on the sand unless an older orca helps them slide back into the water.

or completely different.

Emperor angelfish on the coral reef start out midnight blue with rings of lighter blue. By the time they're adults, they've turned bright sun yellow with deep-blue horizontal stripes. Such coloration in the sea helps camouflage young and adults from attackers and helps each species recognize its own kind.

As soon as they're born, some already know how to swim.

Most walrus calves are born on the ice and can swim and dive almost immediately. In the ocean, baby walruses love to ride on their mothers' backs. Out of water, mothers and babies gather in large "nursery" herds for protection. A mother may even take care of another calf that has lost its own mother.

Others need to learn.

Otter pups are born helpless. A mother otter must teach her baby everything: how to eat prickly sea urchins, crack shellfish with a rock, and fluff its thick fur with air to keep warm. While the pup is still learning, a mother otter will dive with it tucked under her front flipper. When she goes hunting, she wraps her baby in a cradle of kelp so it won't float away.

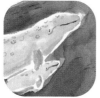

Alone or together, ocean babies travel far to find food...

Gray whale calves drink their mothers' milk during the long swim to cold, northern feeding waters. There, calves stop nursing and learn to suck up food from the ocean bottom. Calves learn many things by mimicking their mothers, who teach and play with them—even "tickling" their young underneath with bubbles from their blowhole.

or wait for food to find them.

As they grow, small predatory tunicates develop special hoods that snap down to trap any food drifting close enough. These creatures live in the sunless deep sea, where many bioluminescent organisms glow in the dark to attract food.

Some change homes like you change clothes.

Hermit crabs must search for ever bigger shells to live in as they grow. Some decorate their shell "houses" with anemones—creating symbiosis where the anemone's sting protects the crab from enemies, and the crab's leftovers become an anemone meal.

Others spend their whole lives in one familiar place.

Most sea anemones rarely travel and must eat by unfurling their stinging tentacles to catch morsels floating by. Certain fish, such as the anemone clownfish, manage to lay their eggs right on the anemone, keeping their young safe from more mobile predators.

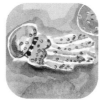

No matter where they live,

Adélie penguin chicks in Antarctica huddle together for shelter against the frigid wind, while their parents go swimming for food. When the parents return, their young ones hungrily gobble down undigested food right from their parents' throat.

what color, shape, or size,

Sea jelly larvae look like tiny flowers hiding in caverns and under rocky ledges. Young jellies reproduce by making exact copies of themselves, splitting in two again and again. Some tiny, some huge, jellies grow to become graceful floaters that drift and pulse on the ocean currents.

 one day ocean babies grow up, just like you will.

Turtle hatchlings, born on the beach, spend their early lives floating on the ocean currents. As adults, sea turtles swim thousands of miles. Female turtles return many times to the beach where they were born to lay their own eggs in the sand.

 Then, big as a bus, and smaller than seeds, billions of *new* babies are born to the ocean — and life begins again.

During their life cycle from babies to adults, ocean animals go through many changes to survive and give birth. Because ocean covers most of our planet, the survival of ocean organisms and their young is vital to human life.

TO LEARN MORE about ocean babies and keeping their ocean world healthy, here are some resources that have links to many others:

American Zoo and Aquarium Association
   (www.aza.org)
Birch Aquarium at Scripps
   (www.aquarium.ucsd.edu)
Marine Activities, Resources
   & Education (MARE),
   UC Berkeley Lawrence Hall of Science
   (www.lawrencehallofscience.org/MARE)

Monterey Bay Aquarium (www.mbayaq.org)
   and Monterey Bay Aquarium Research
   Institute (www.mbari.org)
National Aquarium
   in Baltimore
   (www.aqua.org)
National Marine Educators
   Association
   (www.marine-ed.org)
National Oceanic and Atmospheric
   Administration (www.noaa.gov)
Oceans for Life
   (www.nationalgeographic.com/seas)

To Sarah, who has loved books since she was an ocean baby—DLR

To my brother, Masaki, who taught me so many great things about ocean lives—HN

For encouraging her fascination with the ocean and sharing their expertise on this book, the author wishes especially to thank Brian Gibeson, Marine Biologist, Gibeson Consulting, and Catherine Halversen, Marine Biologist and co-director of Marine Activities, Resources & Education (MARE) at the Lawrence Hall of Science, University of California at Berkeley.

Paintings in this book are watercolor on Arches paper.
Book design by Bea Jackson. The body and display text for the book are set in Cochin.

Library of Congress Cataloging-in-Publication Data
Rose, Deborah Lee.
Ocean babies / by Deborah Lee Rose ; illustrated by Hiroe Nakata.
p. cm.
Summary: Describes baby animals that live in the ocean, pointing out their many differences as well as their most important similarities.
1. Marine animals—Infancy—Juvenile literature. [1. Marine animals.
2. Animals—Infancy.] I. Nakata, Hiroe, ill. II. Title.
QL122.2.R67 2004
591.3'9'09162--dc22
2003014075

ISBN 0-7922-6669-2 (Trade Edition)   ISBN 0-7922-8312-0 (Library Edition)

Printed in the United States of America

One of the world's largest nonprofit scientific and educational organizations, the National Geographic Society was founded in 1888 "for the increase and diffusion of geographic knowledge." Fulfilling this mission, the Society educates and inspires millions every day through its magazines, books, television programs, videos, maps and atlases, research grants, the National Geographic Bee, teacher workshops, and innovative classroom materials. The Society is supported through membership dues, charitable gifts, and income from the sale of its educational products. This support is vital to National Geographic's mission to increase global understanding and promote conservation of our planet through exploration, research, and education. For more information, please call 1-800-NGS-LINE (647-5463) or write to the following address:

NATIONAL GEOGRAPHIC SOCIETY
1145 17th Street N.W.
Washington, D.C. 20036-4688
U.S.A.
Visit the Society's Web site: www.nationalgeographic.com